PAYING TAXES

A TRUE BOOK
by
Sarah De Capua

Children's Press®
A Division of Scholastic Inc.

New York Toronto London Auckland Sydney
Mexico City New Delhi Hong Kong
Danbury, Connecticut

Public libraries are among the services supported by tax money.

Reading Consultant
Nanci R. Vargus, Ed.D.
Teacher in Residence
University of Indianapolis
Indianapolis, Indiana

Author's Dedication:
To Stephen IV

The photograph on the cover shows a woman preparing her taxes. The photograph on the title page shows the United States Capitol in Washington, D.C., where federal tax laws are created.

Library of Congress Cataloging-in-Publication Data
De Capua, Sarah.
    Paying Taxes / by Sarah De Capua.
       p. cm. — (A True book)
    Includes bibliographical references and index
    Summary: Discusses what taxes are, why we pay taxes, and how the government spends taxes.
    ISBN 0-516-22332-1 (lib. bdg.)   0-516-27367-1 (pbk.)
    1. Taxation—United States—Juvenile literature. 2. Taxation—Juvenile literature. [1. Taxation.] I. Title. II. Series.
HJ2381.D4 2002
336.2'00973—dc2   2001047198

Contents

A couple working on their taxes

Paying Taxes

Do the adults you know talk about paying taxes? Have you ever heard a person who is running for public office promise to cut taxes? Did you know that whenever you buy a video game or a compact disc, you pay taxes too?

Local taxes may help pay for such services as garbage pickup.

A tax is the money that people and businesses pay in order to support a government. Taxes pay for the services a government provides.

Three types of government are supported by taxes: local,

state, and federal. Local governments run towns and cities. State government refers to the state where you live. State government business is run in your state's capital city.

State government is supported by state taxes.

The federal government governs the entire United States. Leaders of the federal government work in the nation's capital, Washington, D.C. All three kinds of government receive money from taxes. It takes a lot of tax money to provide services, so people pay a lot of taxes.

Almost everything is taxed. Whenever people buy gasoline, movie tickets, or computer games, they pay taxes. Airline

tickets, telephone calls, and
sometimes clothing and food are
taxed. People pay income tax—
a tax on the money they earn
from their jobs. Property taxes
must be paid when a person
owns property, such as a house.

A highway toll is a type of tax.

Have you ever been riding in a car when the driver had to stop and pay a toll? That toll was a tax. Is your home powered by electricity? Taxes are added to the electric bill. Taxes are also added to your family's phone, gas, and water bills. Even postage stamps are a kind of tax. The stamp you put on a letter helps pay for the services of the post office that will deliver it.

The law says that taxes must be paid. Anyone who does not pay the required amount of tax is breaking the law.

Why Do People Pay Taxes?

Taxes provide services for the community that individuals could not otherwise afford. Taxes pay for our public schools, police and fire services, and public libraries. Taxes also make it possible to have public parks and playgrounds, public transportation, power plants, and

Public schools and public playgrounds are paid for by taxes.

Taxes help maintain
fire services and
highways.

well-maintained roads and highways. Individuals would not be able to enjoy any of these things without the taxes that pay for them.

The word "tax" comes from the Latin word *taxare*, which means "to judge the value of something." Goods and services are taxed by how useful and valuable they are to people. The more valuable a good or service is, the higher its tax. For example, the tax paid for a new car is higher than the tax paid for a new soccer ball.

Taxes have existed for thousands of years. Ever since governments were created, people have paid taxes.

Sometimes people rebel against paying taxes. One of the most famous examples is the Boston Tea Party of 1773. Great Britain had imposed a tea tax on the American colonists and the colonists

Colonists dressed as American Indians dumped tea into Boston Harbor during the Boston Tea Party.

believed the tax was unfair. In protest, a group of Massachusetts colonists dumped a shipload of British tea into Boston Harbor. The colonists' action led to the American Revolutionary War (1775–83)—and independence from Great Britain.

When the colonies became the United States of America, a new government was set up. This government gave American citizens the right to play a part in deciding what should be taxed and how high taxes should be.

Strange Taxes

Throughout history, people have paid taxes that might sound strange today. For example, ancient Romans paid taxes on their togas. During the 1700s, Russian men were required to pay taxes on their beards, and Frenchmen were taxed for their wigs.

A statue of an ancient Roman man in a toga

Wigs were a popular fashion for Frenchmen in the 1700s.

Kinds of Taxes

There are several different kinds of taxes. The amount a person pays for each tax differs, depending on the community or state in which he or she lives.

Perhaps the easiest tax to understand is the sales tax. This tax is paid whenever a

Most items that people buy have a sales tax.

person buys something, such as new sneakers, a videocassette, or a DVD.

People who own land, homes, or other buildings pay a property tax. Other items that sometimes require property taxes are boats, cars, and farm machines.

People who own property have to pay property taxes.

An excise tax is a tax on luxury items that are made in the United States, such as jewelry and furs. Excise taxes may be placed on some items as a kind of penalty for buying them. These items include

alcoholic beverages and ciga-
rettes. The tax is meant to
discourage people from buying
these products.

Tariffs are taxes on products
imported from other countries.
Products that people pay tariffs
on include cars and jewelry.

Tariffs are taxes on
products imported
from other countries,
such as foreign cars.

Everybody who has a job, including doctors, factory workers, and construction workers, pays federal income tax.

The U.S. federal government and many state governments impose an income tax. This is a tax on the amount of money a person earns. Americans who earn the highest incomes pay the highest taxes. Americans who earn the lowest wages pay the lowest taxes.

Besides income tax, two other kinds of taxes are subtracted from a person's earnings. They are the unemployment tax and the social security tax. Both are taxes imposed by the federal government.

The unemployment tax funds a program that provides people who have lost their jobs with a portion of their salary for a

These people are waiting in line to get government unemployment checks.

certain period of time. Social-security taxes support a government program that pays people over age 65 a certain amount of money each month to help pay their expenses.

How Governments Spend Taxes

By looking around your town, you can see how local and state governments spend tax money. Taxes pay for police services, fire services, and public-school education. Tax money also pays for repairing

Local and state government tax
money helps pay for road repairs.

roads and bridges, and maintaining some water systems
and power plants.

Local tax money pays the salaries of police officers, firefighters, librarians, and others. Leaders of local government, such as mayors, are also paid with tax money.

Local governments get most of their money from property taxes. State governments also give money to local governments.

Taxes imposed by state governments pay for services too. These services include building

The salaries of librarians, police officers, and mayors are all paid with local tax money.

and maintaining state highways as well as operating the state government. State taxes also support state colleges and universities. State parks and natural-resource areas are also maintained through taxes. State police officers, the governor, and state senators and representatives are paid with tax money.

The U.S. Constitution gives the federal government the power to collect taxes. The

State taxes support state universities (left) and state parks (below).

United States Congress decides how national tax money will be spent.

Federal taxes pay for running the government in Washington, D.C. Taxes pay the salaries of the president, the vice president, and the people who serve in Congress. Taxes are also used to maintain U.S. military forces and American space-exploration programs. Federal taxes are set aside to aid business and industry throughout the United States.

The salaries of the U.S. president (above left), the vice president (above, second from right), and all other federal government workers are paid with federal tax money. Federal taxes are used to maintain the American space-exploration program (right).

During his presidency, Bill Clinton visited this flooded community and promised to send federal aid for the clean-up effort.

Federal tax money helps states that suffer natural disasters. These include earthquakes, fires, tornadoes, hurricanes, snowstorms, floods, and other devastating events.

Taxes Go Around the World

Americans' tax money isn't used only in the United States. Sometimes the money is used to aid other countries. These other countries may need help establishing industries or cleaning up after a natural disaster. The federal government sends this aid, which can be either money, equipment, or food, to help people in foreign lands.

American supplies being delivered to victims of an earthquake in Turkey

What Makes a Good Tax?

Taxes help people maintain a decent quality of life. However, most people agree that not everything should be taxed. Most people also believe that taxes should not be too high.

In the United States, elected government leaders decide what should be taxed. But these

A politician giving a speech about taxes

leaders represent the views of the people. Citizens can have some effect on tax laws by voting for government leaders who agree with their views.

People must first decide whether a tax is good or bad. They can do this by answering several questions:

Does the tax serve the common good?
This means, does the tax provide a service or support a program that is needed by the community? An example of a tax that brings benefits is the postage stamp. By paying for postage, people help keep the postal service running.

Is the tax fair?
In other words, does the tax apply to everyone in the same way?

A postage stamp on a letter guarantees that the letter will be delivered.

Will everyone be able to pay the tax?

This means, is the tax affordable?

Is the tax easy to collect?

If the tax is easy to collect, the government can be sure it gets its money.

Does the tax help the economy?
The economy is the country's system of industry, trade, and finance. Taxes such as the unemployment tax provide income for people who have lost their jobs. With that money, they can afford to buy food and other things they need. When people have the ability to purchase goods and services, it helps the economy.

In spite of these questions, not everyone agrees on which taxes are good or how high they should be. However,

almost everyone agrees that certain taxes are necessary to provide needed services. People may not always enjoy paying taxes. But obeying the law and paying taxes is part of being a good citizen.

To Find Out More

Here are some additional resources to help you learn more about taxes:

 **Books**

De Capua, Sarah. **Running for Public Office.** Children's Press, 2002.

Lubov, Andrea. **Taxes and Government Spending.** Lerner, 1990.

Quiri, Patricia Ryon. **Congress.** Children's Press, 1998.

Quiri, Patricia Ryon. **The Constitution.** Children's Press, 1998.

Organizations and Online Sites

Department of the Treasury Kids Page
http://www.ustreas.gov/kids

The Department of the Treasury manages federal finances. At its official website, find out more about why people pay taxes, and follow links to related sites.

Internal Revenue Service
http://www.irs.com

The Internal Revenue Service is the government agency that collects taxes. At its site, you can read about state and federal taxes, read answers to FAQs, and more.

Kids Speak Out About Taxes
http://www.intuit.com/turbotax/contests/rules.html

Read what elementary-school students had to say about taxes and how they should be spent. This site contains the results of a contest sponsored by Intuit.

TaxWeb
http://www.taxweb.com

Includes information about taxes and the tax process. Here you can view federal and state tax forms and find answers to FAQs.

U.S. Congress
http://www.Congress.gov

This site includes links to both houses of Congress—the House of Representatives and the Senate. Find out how leaders in Congress are planning to spend Americans' tax money.

Important Words

capital city that is the center of the government of a state or country

citizen member of a particular country

constitution document containing the principles that govern a country or state

devastating having caused complete destruction

import to bring into a place or country from elsewhere

impose to force to accept by legal means

income money that someone earns or receives regularly

individuals single members of a group

luxury something that a person does not really need but that is enjoyable to have

rebel to fight against the government or the people in charge of something

Index

Meet the Author

Sarah De Capua received her master of arts in teaching degree in 1993 and has since been educating children, first as a teacher and currently as an editor and author of children's books. Other books she has written for Children's Press include *Becoming a Citizen, Running for Public Office, Serving on a Jury,* and *Voting* (True Books); *J.C. Watts, Jr.: Character Counts* (Community Builders); and several titles in the Rookie Read-About® Geography series.

Ms. De Capua resides in Colorado.